W9-CSK-797

Colin —

    I hope the drawings in this book will help you to remember fondly your days at Michigan.

Warm Regards!

John Huick

Spring '91

MICHIGAN: A Sketchbook
of University of Michigan
Campus Scenes

Bill Shurtliff

Regency Publishing Company
Saline, Michigan

Copyright © 1988 by Bill Shurtliff
All rights reserved.
No part of this publication
may be reproduced in any
form without prior written
permission of the publisher.

Published by Regency Publishing Company
P.O. Box 42
Saline, MI 48176

ISBN 0-929075-00-5

Manufactured in the United State of America

10 9 8 7 6 5 4 3 2 1

FOR MY MOTHER AND FATHER,
EVELYN AND BILL.

FOREWORD

The campus of the University of Michigan contains images dear to the hearts of many: students and alumni, their families and friends, the GO BLUE football fans who come to town for every game in the fall, and the "townies" who have had the privilege and the predicament of sharing space with this noble institution. For those who attended and lived on campus, as well as for those who simply love the U. of M., this book is intended. As for myself, I was fortunate enough to have had the best of both worlds: the "townie" who grew up to attend the University and then stayed to live in town again. And so, the images in this book from my sketchbooks, while very personal to me, I hope will also be meaningful to you, and perhaps evoke a special memory of a place and time which is particular to the University of Michigan in "dear Ann Arbor town."

Special thanks to my wife, Janet LaBeau, who helped with every aspect of the preparation of this book. And warmest thanks, also, to Bob Bykowski for working with this project, loving it also, and seeing it through to its completion.

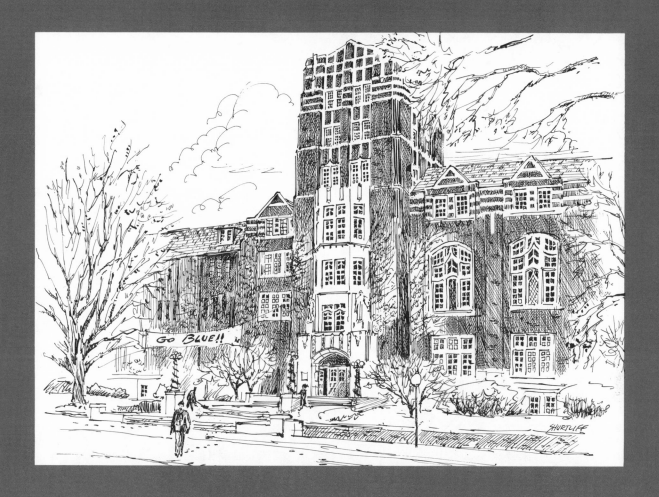

NICKELS ARCADE

ANN ARBOR

SHURTLIFF

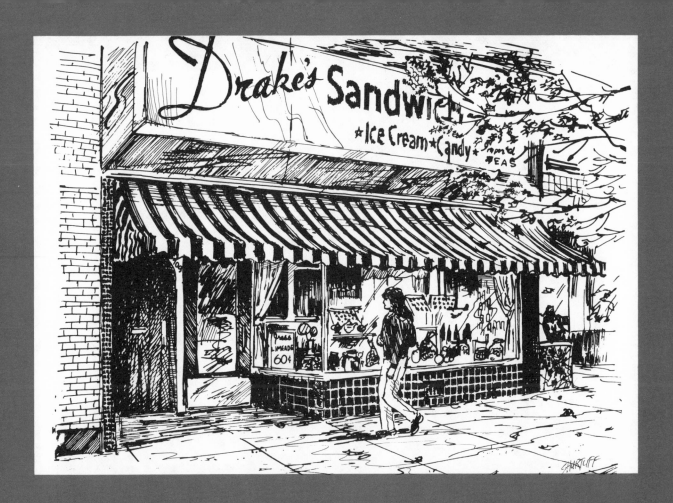

SHURTLIFF
-88-

13

SHURTLIFF
'83   21

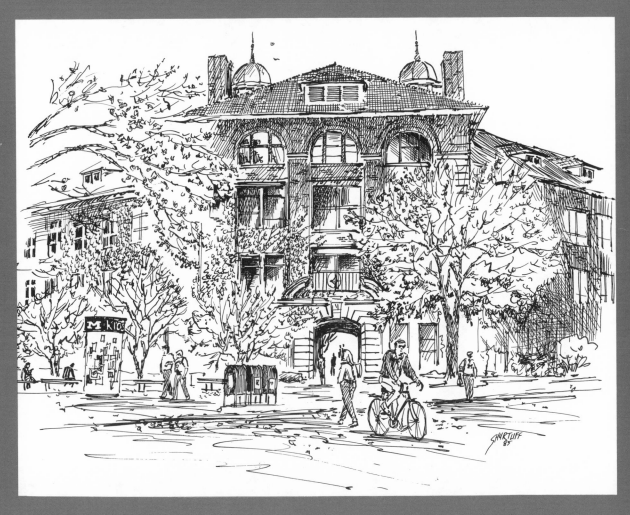

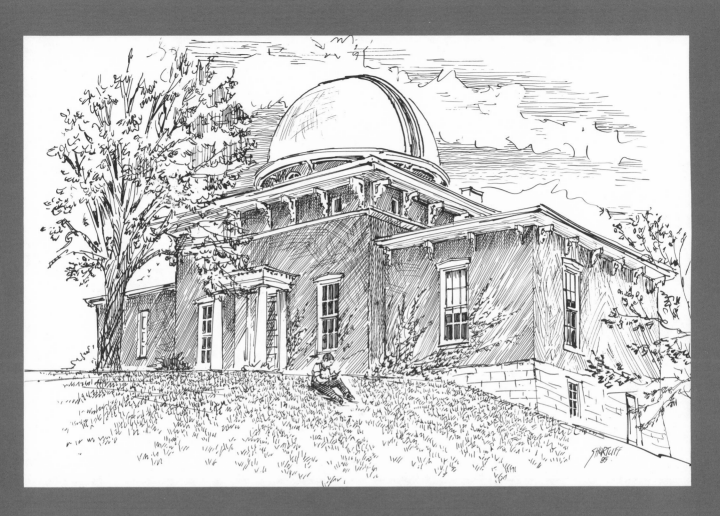

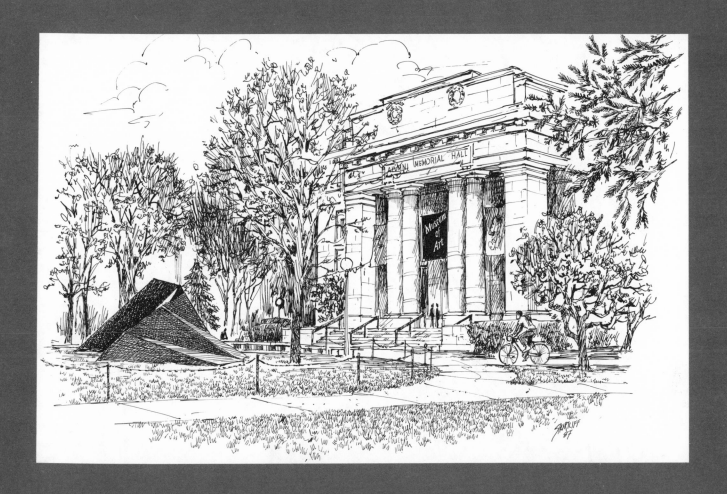

L. CLEMENTS LIBRARY

SHURTLIFF

NEWSPAPERS
MAGAZINES
PAPER BACK BOOKS
ES MODELS
SUPPLIES
ILETRIES

Repsi

Pepsi

BLUE FRONT

BLUE
FRONT

Coca Cola

RALPHS

MARKET

OPEN

SHURTLIFF

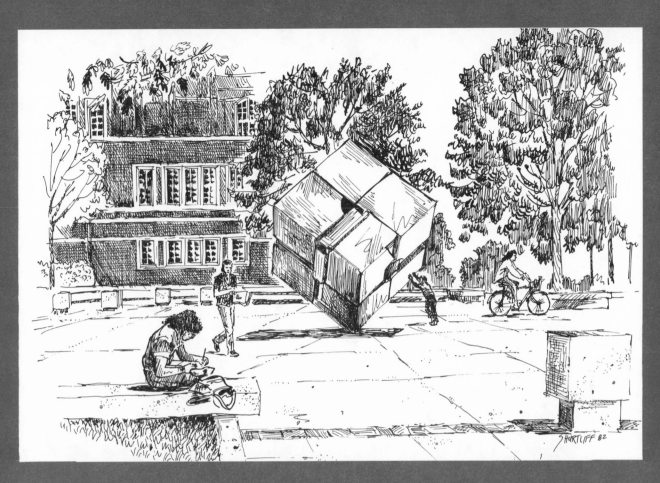

Following are identifications of the buildings and scenes in these drawings. For information on the history of these buildings, consult: *A Guide to the Campus of the University of Michigan* by Margo MacInnes, (The University of Michigan Press, 1978); *Historic Buildings: Ann Arbor, Michigan* by the Ann Arbor Historic District Commission, 1977; or *Historical Notes to Accompany Bill Shurtliff's U. of M. Sketchbook* by Janet LaBeau, (Regency, 1988).

ABOUT THE ARTIST

Bill Shurtliff was born in Ann Arbor and spent his boyhood playing in many of the same places which the drawings in this book depict. He received a Bachelor of Fine Arts, with honors, from the University of Michigan School of Art in 1976. Though he continues to paint and sculpt, he is perhaps better known for his pen and ink drawings. Reviewers have admired Mr. Shurtliff's work for the "delicacy" of his lines and the "significant" detailing. His drawings are featured regularly in the *Ann Arbor News* and in many University of Michigan publications.

Although the subject matter of his artwork varies widely and certainly extends beyond the campus and town, it is with special love and appreciation that Bill Shurtliff continues to sketch and reflect the images of Ann Arbor, this place which so many of us find very special indeed.